The Redemption of Eve

A True Story of Redemption, Healing,
and Divine Encounters Through
the Courts of Heaven

By

Stephanie Stanfill

The Redemption of Eve

A True Story of Redemption, Healing,
and Divine Encounters Through
the Courts of Heaven

By

Stephanie Stanfill

theredemptionofeve.com
stephanie@theredemptionofeve.com

The Redemption of Eve

A True Story of Redemption, Healing, and Divine Encounters Through the Courts of Heaven

Copyright © 2025 Stephanie Stanfill

Scroll Publishers
PO Box 5847
Pinehurst, NC 28374 USA

Additional copies available.

Contact: stephanie@theredemptionofeve.com

ISBN 13 TP: 978-1-962808-24-8
ISBN 13 eBook: 978-1-962808-25-5

Cover Design by Darian Horner Design
(www.darianhorner.com)
Image: 123rf.com #242492550

First Edition: July 2025

10 9 8 7 6 5 4 3 2 1 0

Printed in the United States of America

Table of Contents

Acknowledgments

For my beautiful daughters, Angelina and Rachael. You have always had my heart.

For my mom, Pat, and second mama, Linda, thank you for your love and support.

Dr. Ron and Adina Horner, words cannot express my thanks for your obedience, sacrifices, support, and love.

To my best friend, Marcelina, I am honored to have been on this journey with you as a friend who sticks closer than a brother. Thank you from the bottom of my heart.

Finally, to the back porch girls, we are forever friends with mansions on the same cove in Heaven. Thank you for doing Heaven with me on earth!

Foreword

Over the last few years, I have been honored to have Stephanie Stanfill in my life. She served as my Executive Assistant and is now the Chief Operating Officer in the ministry my wife and I steward, where she has made a profound contribution. I have watched her grow by leaps and bounds during this time and have encouraged her to begin writing and expressing the things inside her.

This book is the first of many that I expect her to write. She has discovered the faithfulness of our Heavenly Father and has sought to live out the mandate of her life. Her road has been bumpy, but the wonderful thing is that our heavenly Father has been faithful to Stephanie, bringing her through the ups and downs of life. Her beautiful daughters are a testament to her life of promises made and fulfilled.

May you find encouragement as you read this account of the Father's never-failing goodness and how he fulfills His promises. As further testimony, Stephanie just closed on her new home this morning, the day I am writing this foreword. This is another testimony of God's goodness. May you experience the same.

Dr. Ron M. Horner

Pastor and Author

— ∞ —

Call to Me, and I will answer you, and show you great and mighty things, which you do not know. (Jeremiah 33:3, NKJV)

These words from the heart of God beckon us to seek Him, to step into the unknown with faith, and to discover the depths of His love and purpose. In *The Redemption of Eve*, Stephanie Stanfill responds to this divine invitation with courage, vulnerability, and unwavering trust in the transformative power of God's grace. Her journey, as shared in these pages, is a testament to the truth that when we call upon Him, He reveals mysteries that heal, restore, and redeem. Stephanie's story is one of raw honesty, tracing a path through the shadows of generational sin, personal struggles, and the weight of shame to the radiant light of God's redemptive love. It is a narrative that echoes Colossians 3:13:

Forgive one another if any of you has a grievance against someone. Forgive as the Lord forgave you. (NIV)

Through her encounters in the Courts of Heaven, Stephanie unveils the power of forgiveness—not just for others, but for herself and her lineage, breaking the chains that have bound generations. Her experiences remind us that forgiveness, rooted in Christ's own sacrifice, is the key to freedom, allowing us to step into the fullness of God's promises.

This book is not merely a recounting of one woman's spiritual odyssey; it is an invitation for you, the reader, to call upon God and witness the "great and mighty things" He longs to show you. It challenges us to forgive as we have been forgiven, to seek intimacy with our Creator, and to reclaim the honor lost in the Garden. As you turn these pages, may you be inspired to step boldly into your own heavenly encounters, trusting that the Father's love surpasses every past mistake and every generational burden. May you, like Stephanie, find your way back to Eden, where honor is restored, and God's presence is as near as your next breath.

Neal Jackson
Pastor and Author

— ∞ —

It's an extraordinary thing to walk through life with someone for over 30 years. To witness the seasons—joy and heartbreak, laughter and tears, births and losses, setbacks and comebacks. I've had the honor of doing just that with the author of this book—my best friend, sister in Christ, prayer and podcast partner! We've weathered storms together: Marriages, divorces, deaths of husbands, raising teenagers (that one almost got us!). Growth that came with pain, and transformation that only comes through surrender. I have watched her manage a whole household while attending college and earning her degree. Stephanie's fierce determination is written throughout her DNA. She has become a powerful woman of God—a governing son in the Kingdom. She is one of the most relentless and courageous women I have ever known.

The Redemption of Eve is not just a book. It is a lifeline. It is raw, honest, and unfiltered—written from the depths of a woman who knows what it means to fall, to rise, and to be redeemed. This is her offering to those who feel stuck in the in-between, trapped in the pain, or uncertain if they'll ever see the other side. In these pages, you will find the truth. You will find hope. And you will hear the voice of someone who has lived out every word she writes. I couldn't be prouder of her, and I couldn't be more honored to introduce you to this work. My prayer is that it meets you right where you are—and that, like her, you too find your redemption.

Love Has No Secrets,
Marcelina Angelina

— ∞ —

It is my great pleasure to recommend this book to you. I have known Stephanie for quite some time now, yet I did not know her in her earlier days. What I can tell you is that she is the real deal in her relationship and walk with our Savior.

I can say she hasn't lost her edge; however, now her edge is entirely under the blood of Jesus, and so are her many gifts and talents. What blesses me is that she is very transparent about her past, yet she does not wear her past like a badge of honor. She has learned and continues to realize that our journey isn't about us, but rather about Jesus and Him alone.

I encourage you to consider her journey, both good and bad, and take from it the message that God has something very special in store for you, if you put Him first in all things. The truth is that we cannot help but change once we see ourselves as Father sees us. This is what Stephanie did and how she continues to walk in His light day by day.

My blessing is that I get to see the Lord use the fine sandpaper on her to shine her up and perhaps take her where few have ever gone. Yes, we have all failed; however, it is our choice whether we let those failures define us or set those failures aside and walk in God's plan for our lives.

While God may use each of us in a slightly different way, the way God is using Stephanie today should be an encouragement to all of us to strive for greater things, if we do it in His power and strength.

Dr. Robert Rodich
Author

— ∞ —

With deep honor and heartfelt gratitude for my dear friend—someone whose insight and compassion have profoundly shaped my understanding of generational iniquities and curses. This is not just a book. It is a revelation—a powerful work born from the depths of spiritual discernment, prayer, and lived experience. The patterns, struggles, and strongholds that seem to pass from one generation to the next often go unaddressed because we don't realize their spiritual roots. But through countless conversations, teachings, and shared moments of discovery, Stephanie helped me to peel back the layers and see how these unseen forces can shape families, relationships, and destinies.

The wisdom in these pages is not theoretical. It comes from a place of deep study, spiritual authority, and compassionate ministry. Stephanie has spent years walking alongside individuals and families, helping them recognize hidden cycles, break destructive patterns, and step into freedom through the power of Jesus Christ. This book brings that same ministry to your hands—it's clear, practical, and deeply anointed.

What sets this book apart is its balance of biblical truth, personal testimony, and spiritual strategy. The author doesn't just explain what generational iniquities are—she shows us how to identify them, why they matter, and what we can do to walk in victory. It speaks to both the mind and the spirit, and it brings light to places that have been dark for far too long.

I am genuinely excited about the release of this book because I know it has the potential to change lives. My prayer is that as you read, you will experience the same clarity, healing, and empowerment that I did. You'll see your story—and your family's story—through a new lens. You'll discover that you are not powerless. You are chosen, equipped, and called to break cycles and leave a new legacy.

To my friend—the author—thank you. Thank you for your obedience, your boldness, and your love. May this book reach the hearts it was written for, and may it bear fruit for generations to come.

With love and deep respect,

Julie Cox
Pastor,
East Bay Worship Center

Preface

A Journey Back to Eden

Hey friend,

Can we talk honestly for a minute? I mean really honestly—the kind of conversation you'd have over coffee with someone you trust completely.

Have you ever felt that pulling toward something you knew wasn't good for you? That whisper in your mind that makes you second-guess everything you know is right? I'm sitting here thinking about Eve in that garden, and I can't help but wonder what was going through her mind. Was it just one moment of weakness, or had she been wrestling with those thoughts for days? And where was Adam in all of this?

I'll be completely transparent with you—I used to be pretty mad at Eve. I mean, thanks a lot, right? But lately, I've been wondering if there might be more to her story than we've given her credit for. What if there's actually redemption in her story that we've been missing all along?

I've spent way too many years giving in to temptation myself, and for the longest time, I thought it meant I was just weak or broken somehow. Maybe you've felt that way too? Growing up in church, attending Christian school, and having parents who stayed together—I had all the "right" ingredients for a strong faith. But somehow, I still kept messing up, over and over again.

Here's what I used to think: God was this distant figure in the sky, just waiting for me to screw up so He could point out all my failures. By high school, I was fairly certain I'd already blown my chances with him, so why not just give up trying? Sound familiar?

But here's the beautiful thing—Jesus never gave up on me. He kept showing up in the most unexpected ways, even when I was at my absolute worst. And one day, I made a decision that changed everything. I decided to stop putting God in a box. I chose to believe that the same God who spoke to people in the Bible could speak to me, too, right here, right now.

What I'm about to share with you might sound a little wild, but stay with me. This book is full of actual encounters I've had with Heaven—real conversations with Jesus, moments spent in His presence, meetings with people from the Bible, and loved ones who've gone before us. And the crazy part? You don't have to be perfect to experience this. You don't even have to be dead!

I know that might sound too good to be true, but I promise you it's not. God created these heavenly dimensions for intimacy with Him, for healing, for transformation, for truth. Your imagination isn't something to be ashamed of—it's actually one of the ways He designed to connect with you.

So here's my invitation to you: Come on this journey with me. Let's go back to Eden together and discover what God has been trying to show us all along. His love for you is bigger than your worst mistakes, stronger than your deepest shame, and more patient than you could ever imagine.

He's been waiting for you, friend. Not the perfect version of you—the real you, right where you are today.

Are you ready to see what He has in store?

With so much love,
Stephanie Stanfill

Chapter 1:

The Journey

You know what keeps me up at night sometimes? I wonder how someone finds their way back from rock bottom. I think about Eve a lot—can you imagine going from walking with God in perfect harmony to...well, everything that came after? How do you rebuild your life when everything you've known has crumbled? When marriages fall apart, relationships die, and you're left standing in the wreckage of what used to be your life.

And here's the really hard part—how do the people who knew you "before" ever trust the "new" you? When they've seen you at your absolute worst, can they believe transformation is even possible? I wrestle with this every single day.

I have something special for you to do. The road will be hard and tough. "The effectual fervent prayers of a righteous man avail much." (James 5:16)

This journey with Jesus? It's been the hardest thing I've ever done, and also the most worth it. I'm not going to sugarcoat what's coming in these pages—we're talking about loss, betrayal, murder, alcoholism, idolatry, incest, adultery, and pretty much every sexual sin you can think of. But we're also talking about redemption, face-to-face encounters with angels, heavenly encounters, conversations with loved ones who have gone before us, and, yes, even Jesus Himself.

I want you to know that if God can reach me in the mess I was in, He can reach you, too. He really doesn't play favorites.

Let me paint you a picture of who I used to be. I was the person everyone could count on to be...well, a hot mess. Loud, angry, drunk, dishonest—making terrible decisions that hurt everyone around me while claiming to be a Christian. And not just any Christian—I was the "spirit-filled" kind who spoke in tongues and went to church while being a drunk mom, wife, friend, sister, and daughter. Yeah, I was that contradiction walking around.

I wonder sometimes—when Adam first saw Eve, she was perfect, right? But after that whole apple situation went down, did he look at her differently? Did he blame her in his heart, even though the Bible tells us he was standing right there with her? Did she carry shame because of his looks, or did he actually make her feel ashamed?

What about you? How much shame are you carrying around?

I'll never forget this one moment that hit me like a brick wall. I was working as an Executive Director for a nonprofit, and I had brought in this amazing friend to help with a city project. She had skills I desperately needed—I'm the big-picture visionary type, and she was the one who could actually make things happen. We were planning this huge city-wide event, and she was at a local football game, telling someone about our project. This well-meaning person said, "Oh, I know exactly who can help you with this, but here's the thing—you either love her or you hate her."

They were talking about me. That's how people saw me. The shame hit me so hard I could barely breathe.

Here's the thing—I thought I was this no-nonsense, strong, assertive businesswoman. A successful mom of four, a good wife, a loyal friend. But really? I was just a fake. At least, that's what I thought until God started showing me who He says I am. What do you think He says about you?

February 8, 2021, Journal Entry

I had a vision of a large table in front of me, and I heard, "I have prepared a table for you in the presence of your enemies." I saw Jesus slip a large, purple signet ring on my middle finger. He hugged me and placed His hand on my chest. He reminded me of an encounter a few days prior, where I had seen the Holy Spirit put His hand on me, saying, "It is complete."

This same evening, I attended a Sedar. I was new at visually seeing the realms of Heaven, but as I took the bread and wine, my vision opened up, and Jesus was walking towards me. He sat in the chair next to me, in the natural setting, and took communion with me.

Haggai 2:23

I will make you like a signet ring on my finger, says the Lord, for I have chosen you. I, the Lord of Heaven's Armies, have spoken! (NLT)

I can't help but wonder about Eve's pain after everything fell apart. When her son Abel was murdered, who was pointing fingers at her? Was Adam blaming her for the fall that led to this tragedy? Was he able to honor her in her grief, or was he too wrapped up in his guilt and shame? Can you imagine the agony—remembering the perfect garden while grieving your murdered child? With so few people on earth, why was there already so much dishonor and blame?

Which brings me back to the question that haunts me: How do you walk in newness when your past is so ugly? How do people trust you when they know where you've been?

Let me be brutally honest with you. Between the ages of twenty-three and thirty-three, I was running around telling everyone what a "survivor" I was, when I was a complete fraud. I was knee-deep in every sin you can imagine, and it didn't matter that I claimed to be saved—I wanted what I wanted.

During this time, I married a full-blown alcoholic who was seventeen years older than I. He eventually died from the very disease I ended up developing myself. Yes, you read that right—I became the very thing I used to judge. I married him, trying to fill this massive daddy-shaped hole in my heart, and it led to ten brutal years of uncertainty, abuse, lies, and failure.

But here's what I need you to understand—it wasn't all his fault. I've had to face the role I played in that toxic mess. This man loved me, even through his disease. I felt it during his sober moments. He loved our children fiercely, and he loved Jesus too. So why did it all go so wrong? Why did dishonor, shame, death, and failure show up so early in my story?

I eventually turned to Jesus, begging for answers, and I received some. But then I fell even harder after my husband died. I "survived" only to keep failing over and over again.

February 12, 2021, Journal Entry

During praise and worship, I saw myself on my knees in front of Him (The Father). He took my hand, pulled me close, put me on his lap, and I lay across his chest, hugging Him. I was given Psalm 91.

Here's another question that keeps me awake: How are my children ever supposed to trust again? Not just me, but God? Not just God, but life itself? I've been the absolute worst example of Christian living. Even though I love them with every fiber of my being, they've been exposed to so much dysfunction and pain. They've lived through the death of a parent, abuse, religious hypocrisy, abandonment, alcoholism, and a whole list of other failures and heartaches.

The guilt and shame from that? It's overwhelming. They saw me try to protect them when I couldn't even protect myself. They saw a mother who loved deeply but also carried massive arrogance, which brought them humiliation. I wonder if Eve walked in this same kind of shame after the fall. Or maybe it's just me—do most of us put this burden on ourselves?

I don't pretend to have all the answers. The only thing I know for certain is this: I AM new. Walking it out, trying to prove it? Well, maybe I'm not supposed to prove anything. Maybe I'm just supposed to be. Be fulfilled and made whole by the only One who can do that. Be His. Be still and know. Be quiet.

February 16, 2021, Journal Entry

I heard the Lord say, "You are my daughter. I want the very best for you. I love you. You will walk through this, and it will test you, but like the refiners' fire, I will mold you with my very hands. You will be the tool, a weapon I have created to crush the enemy. Many people will come to see and learn. I prophesy change, deliverance, assurance, prosperity, and governing. My hand will be upon you and with you. You will deliver many from the pit and storm. Truth will be on your tongue. Be anxious for nothing, for nothing comes from that, but in all things, follow My heart, my longing. Follow My precepts. Think bigger. Think Big. Don't lose heart. Stand firm. Oh, precious one, I have longed for this day. I am not done. Don't turn to the left or the right. Face Me. I will clear your path. I will make the way straight. I will put upon your lips, fire! Change! I will pour out love! Heart, soul, and body will be touched. Healed! Blessings! Honor! Conditions are right! You will exercise the blood. You know the power, use it. Don't hold back. Don't let go of its power. Don't let go of the hem of My garment. Trust ME. Trust IN Me. Favor upon favor upon favor. Walk in truth and light will shine. My precepts will be your precepts. Line upon line, tittle upon tittle, you will walk with fire, anointed by My hand. You will walk in truth. You will walk in boldness. Fire upon your hands and heart, beating for Me. For ME. For My people. Love shines down on you. Love straight from My throne. You will love others. You know my strength and will walk in it, Proclaim it! Proclaim these things and they will come to pass."

Note: 'You will walk through this, and it will test you.' This has happened and still is! Regarding the rest of the journal entry, I have begun working for an international ministry. I am walking out this word from the Lord, even now!

Today is a new day. I am a new person. I feel it in every waking moment. I wish I could pour this newness into my daughters, show them it's real, and wash away all the horrible memories of the past. I wish I could go back in time and redo it all for them, so when I say "I'm new, trust me. Trust what I'm doing and trust Him," they would actually believe me. But broken trust is precisely that—broken. Did Eve feel like she had shattered Adam's trust? Did she carry that blame, or did he make sure she felt it?

Isaiah 54:4

You will no longer remember the shame of your youth (NLT)

This scripture is what my Father (and yes, I call Him Father now—it's a choice I make willingly every day) gave me years ago. He's become exactly that to me—my Father.

I began examining the patterns in my life, and I realized there was a consistent theme: dishonor. Isn't that fascinating? How does dishonor work? How does it follow you around? Can you trace it through your family line? Did Eve feel like she was the reason dishonor entered humanity? Did she feel dishonored by Adam or by her children?

Let's take a moment to consider this. If Adam was standing right next to Eve when she ate the apple, but Scripture tells us sin entered through Adam, then why do we blame her for bringing dishonor to mankind? Did she believe that, too? Do you?

Romans 5:12

Death through Adam, life through Christ.

Therefore, just as sin entered the world through one man, and death through sin, and in this way death came to all people because all sinned. (NIV)

Here's what I've learned: When you've been dishonored, you tend to dishonor others. When you dishonor, you will be dishonored in return. It's this vicious cycle of reaping and sowing.

Where did dishonor start in my life? Honestly, I can't pinpoint it. Family dynamics are complicated for everyone, aren't they? Dynamically loving yet destructive, disheartening, and sometimes devastating. I'm not unique in this—most of us have similar stories. This is why we must examine generational patterns and break the cycles.

February 18, 2021, Journal Entry from Heaven

I was praying about loving people. It isn't my strong suit. I saw a picture in my mind of Jesus standing before me. He was holding a huge heart. It looked like a Valentine's Day heart, but it was big. He was putting the last of the pieces together. The heart was multicolored with pink, white, and red. You could see the multiple scars from where it had been fragmented. He was putting the last few pieces back together at the very bottom. He was smiling. The heart hovered in front of Him. Then, in praise and worship, I felt the Holy Spirit put His hand in mine and breathe on me.

Friend, if you're reading this and recognizing yourself in my story, please know you're not alone. The journey from brokenness to wholeness is messy and hard, but it's also the most beautiful thing you'll ever experience. God is in the business of putting hearts back together, one scarred piece at a time.

Chapter 2:
Family Secrets

Can we talk about something that might make you a little uncomfortable? I want to discuss generational curses—or, as I prefer to call them, generational consequences. I know, I know, some of you might be thinking, "But Jesus broke all that stuff!" And you're not wrong but stick with me here because this conversation might change how you see your family patterns.

Let me clear something up right from the start. When I talk about generational curses, I'm not saying God is up there cursing family lines. That's not how our loving Father works. What I'm talking about is more like...well, think of it as family patterns that get passed down. The consequences of choices, behaviors, and sins ripple through generations like stones thrown in a pond.

Most of us have heard about sowing and reaping, right?

Galatians 6:7-8

⁷ Do not be deceived, God is not mocked; for whatever a man sows, that he will also reap. ⁸ For he who sows to his flesh will of the flesh reap corruption, but he who sows to the Spirit will of the Spirit reap everlasting life.

Growing up Baptist, we didn't often discuss these topics. But let me tell you, these generational patterns are more real than you might think. Sexual sin, addiction, abuse, adultery—these things have a way of showing up generation after generation, tearing families apart decade after decade.

Here's my challenge to you (and I'm being completely serious): What family secret does your family carry? I dare you to look. Actually, I triple-dog dare you—and yes, I'm going full playground challenge on you here. Can you see patterns? Are you maybe living out a secret yourself right now?

Before you get defensive, this isn't about shame. This is about uncovering things so we can heal them. Healing is precisely how I became new. Want to know how? I started looking both inward and backward. I began examining my family dynamics through what my Heavenly Father was revealing to me, as well as through a concept known as the Courts of Heaven. I'm still on this journey, but breaking those generational consequences from my bloodline has been life-changing.

Let's take a closer look for a moment. Have you ever noticed how certain things seem to follow families? Perhaps it's the way you walk (and sometimes that's quite endearing). I've always slept with my arms above my head, and guess what? So do my daughters. That's harmless, but what about the not-so-harmless stuff?

Strange accidents that keep happening in your family line? Businesses that always seem to fail? Marriage after marriage falling apart? Are there certain diseases that appear generation after generation? Financial disasters that hit just when you think you're finally getting ahead?

Have you ever discovered something that happened to your great-grandpa or great-great-grandma that somehow seems to be affecting your life now? These similarities aren't just coincidences, friend, I assure you. They're real, and they follow generations.

I know this can feel overwhelming, but it doesn't have to be. That's why I want you to continue this journey back to Eden with me. We can discover a place of freedom together. You know what they say—we become experts in our trauma, as long as we make it out the other side. My wonderful friend Dr. Ron Horner always says, "If you're going through hell, keep going till you get out the other side."

February 20th, 2021, Journal Entry

I am here, and I am with you always. I am in everything. Look around at the goodness. Look. You may not feel My presence, but I am here, always. Continue to follow Me. I will take you places you've never been. Seek Me, I am here. Forget not who created you. Stand with Me. I am doing something so big. Let your light shine bright to others. They will see Me too. I am taking you places, spiritually, that you have not been before. Places unique just for you. Deep places. Good places. Come deeper every time. Daily. Precept upon precept, line upon line. Walk with Me. You're good enough, you're strong enough, you've endured enough. You've always been enough. Come to Me, all who are weary and heavy laden, and I will give you rest." (Matthew 11:28)

(Note: "I will take you places you've never been." I have been amazed at the places He has taken me in the Spirit! The intimacy is so beautiful.)

Let me tell you about my journey with Jesus. I've been a "Christian" since I was four years old. Man, did I love Jesus! I talked to Him all the time. I'll never forget the time he came into my bathroom when I was little. I was in the bathtub playing with these rubber duckies that looked like Bert and Ernie from Sesame Street (yes, I'm dating myself here), and He walked right into that room. I heard Him ask, clear as day, "Stephanie, will you follow me?"

Without even thinking about it, I said, 'Yes!' From that day on, I felt this incredible pull toward those little prayer benches at the front of our church. I loved those things and felt "called" to them. I actually got baptized at least three times because I felt Jesus so strongly every single time! I still laugh thinking about my sweet little preacher who was patient enough to keep baptizing this enthusiastic little girl over and over again. How precious was he to never scold me for that?

We attended a small Southern Baptist church, and I was always deeply moved by the sermons. It's funny because people said the pastor wasn't even that great of a preacher, but sometimes I would cry and couldn't even tell you why. Can you believe that? Being moved to tears by sermons at such a young age?

I loved my church, my friends, and that sweet pastor. But I was also "moved" by something else—boys. Yes, I was boy-crazy from a young age. Little did I know, I came from a long line of boy-crazy girls and girl-crazy boys. This pattern had a hold on me that was way stronger than I understood at the time. This was a generational iniquity, and it drove me to be and do things I wouldn't have otherwise done.

Now, let me explain something important. Sin is sin—we all know that. However, there is a distinction between sin and iniquity, and understanding this difference has changed everything for me.

Psalms 32:5

I acknowledged my sin to you and did not cover up my iniquity. I said, 'I will confess my transgressions to the LORD.' (NIV)

Here's the difference: Sin means missing the mark. It's doing something against God or another person, doing the opposite of what's right, doing something that will have negative consequences, or failing to do something you know is right. Sin is anything that "falls short of the glory of God." It leads to this downward spiral that, without the Holy Spirit's restoring power, we all tend toward. Every human being born since Adam and Eve has this sinful nature.

But iniquity? That's deeper. Iniquity is a premeditated choice—it's continuing in sin without repentance. When someone commits an iniquity, they're choosing to continue down that path. Left unchecked, it leads to willful sin with no fear of God.

Think about Adam and Eve's family line for a minute. How many people in their generational line died at the hands of another person? Since we all come from them, murder is literally in all of our generational lines. When you look at the world around us, you can see that particular sin playing itself out everywhere. Doesn't that make you curious about why it's so important to uncover and break these patterns?

Do you feel like you've always been set apart? Different somehow? I always knew I was different. During those brutal formative years—second through sixth grade—I felt like a complete outcast. Finding friends was nearly impossible. Girls can be absolutely the worst to each other during those years, and that breaks my heart. We should be building each other up, but instead, we're often experts at tearing each other down.

I was overweight, shy, unsure of myself, and felt like I couldn't learn what was being taught. I felt lost most of the time. Teachers back then didn't know that some students can't understand unless it's taught in their specific "learner language." I'm a visual learner, but there weren't many teachers who could paint a picture for me to understand. It wasn't their fault—they taught according to how they were trained, and I just didn't get it.

Those younger years were pretty sad. I was sad. And then another terrible thing happened when I was in sixth grade—something that shows how generational iniquity can open doors for trauma.

My mom took me to a summer camp run by a well-known organization (I won't name them here). I was molested by one of the leaders. She took me and another little girl into the bathroom while everyone else was elsewhere. I had no idea what was happening and was completely confused and scared.

But God miraculously intervened that day. My mom showed up early, and I started hearing them calling my name over the loudspeaker. I was so grateful to be leaving that space. I often think about that other precious little girl who was left behind with that predator. What happened to her? Was she able to escape? I begged my mom never to take me back there, and thankfully, I never had to go back.

How was this connected to generational sin and iniquity? Well, let me tell you. I wasn't the first in my family line to be molested. Sexual sin is the number one weapon the enemy uses—it either comes to traumatize you or to make you fall. My grandfather brought pornography into our region. He trafficked it, he consumed it, and it became an open door for perversion to enter my family line. That open door led to what happened to me.

Here's something interesting about how I learn and how God speaks to me. As I mentioned, I'm a visual learner. The Lord uses pictures, imagery, dreams, and visions to communicate with me. My visions of Heaven and my many dreams have painted beautiful pictures of understanding for me.

As a young girl, I often saw demonic things. I'm not sure if you can relate, but I had no framework for understanding any of that. We Baptists didn't talk about things like spiritual warfare, remember? When I tried to tell my mom, she said I had a very active imagination instead of helping me understand what was happening. She wasn't trying to dismiss me—she didn't know either. She wasn't taught about these things.

This left me feeling unheard and scared that something was wrong with me. None of my friends at church could understand what I was experiencing either. They looked at me as if I were crazy. Was I?

February 21st, 2021, Journal Entry

Oh, daughter, you are my gift. I will use you for the masses, straight from my throne—power, authority, and wisdom. Let your light shine. Comfort, joy, and peace shall be your dwelling. You have given up so much for the Kingdom, and the Kingdom rewards you shall have. I am your dwelling place, your hiding place. Joy unspeakable, wrapped in My glory, crowned with righteousness, glowing splendor, forever marked. Use this time wisely, and I will bring wisdom. Focus on My heart, for My heart I bring. Charity will be your brand. Clarity befalls you, sealed, marked for My good, for My glory. Waste not this time. Lay down your heart. Judgment will fall this day, this night, but not you. Freedom shall be on your lips. Tongues wag at the darkness, I am the light. Show them the way. Mercies upon mercies are given to you this day. Freedom upon freedom, MARK My words. Solutions, Wisdom, and character will it bring. Thought-provoking speech shall be upon your lips. Tried and true are you. Profit not the prophet, but a prophet shall you be. A mouthpiece for joy unspeakable and life eternal. Bathed in My glory shall you come. Rise up, oh daughter, hear My name. (Oh, Holy One of Israel) Call upon Me and I will be there. Psalms 16: You will make known to me the path of life. In your presence is fullness of joy. At your right hand, there are pleasures forevermore.

Friend, if any of this is resonating with you, please know that you're not alone. The journey of uncovering and breaking generational patterns isn't easy, but it's so worth it. God wants to heal not just you, but your entire family line. He wants to turn your family's story from one of repeated trauma and failure into one of redemption and breakthrough.

The patterns that your family has followed don't have to be followed by your children. That's the beautiful hope we have in Jesus—we can be the generation that says, "enough is enough" and breaks the cycle. We can be the ones who choose healing over hiding, freedom over fear, and truth over family secrets.

Are you ready to take that step with me?

Chapter 3:

Not the Norm

You know that moment when you realize you're just not like everyone else? When I was growing up, I had this lightbulb moment: I didn't have to follow the norm, and honestly, why should I? Looking back now, I can see this was rebellion kicking in—and guess what? Rebellion is likely in your family's generational line as well.

Since I wasn't "normal" anyway, I decided to fight to be different in every way possible. A different look, a different attitude, a different everything. All this did was make my parents even more frustrated with who I was becoming. They wanted compliance—a sweet, rule-following little angel they could be proud of. Who wouldn't want that, right? Well, that didn't happen. I rebelled more and more and more.

I can't blame them for how they felt. Now that I'm a mom myself, I completely understand. When you're going through your own hardships—trying to survive as a person, a mom, building a career, being a wife—you need your kids to cooperate. We lived in the "suck it up, buttercup" era, where keeping the kids quiet was priority number one when times got tough.

My real journey into rebellion started when I was fourteen. There was this boy—isn't there always a boy in these stories? He was the son of our church secretary. I thought, "Why couldn't he be 'the one'?" After all, he kept telling me I was "the one" repeatedly.

This is where things get really interesting, and where the generational sins and iniquities we discussed began to show up in my life in a significant way. This is where dishonor really took root.

Let me ask you something: How does someone dishonor another person? What is dishonor? The dictionary defines it as "a state of shame or disgrace," or to "bring shame or disgrace on someone," or "fail to observe or respect an agreement or principle."

If I'm being honest, I had already been dishonored before this boy even came into the picture, right? These patterns originate from generational sins and iniquities. I'm not going to give you a laundry list of all my family's failures—adultery, sexual sins, molestation, silencing—but that's where it all started. It started there with you, too.

These things affected me generationally, and they're affecting you generationally too. Now, I'm not saying we can blame our families for our adult choices—we have to own our decisions. But I am asking this: What's the root? It's sin and iniquity that runs through the generational line, and we end up living in the consequences of it.

You can bet I picked up that baton and started running my own race of dishonor. There's truth in what the Bible says about dishonoring your parents—it brings a whole other set of problems to the family line, and you end up dishonoring yourself in the process.

Here's what I learned: If you feel dishonored, you'll take on dishonor as an identity without even realizing it. I lived it. I drew it into myself. I became dishonored.

March 13th, 2021, Journal Entry

In praise and worship, I saw myself standing before Jesus. I knelt before Him and He came to me, wrapped his arms around me. I began to see a bubble above my head as if I were in a cartoon, like when the cartoon person was thinking. Jesus took his hand and swept the bubble with the thoughts away. I told him I was laying idols down and that I needed help with that.

I could go on and on about the messy details of my life of dishonor. I could tell you stories about being okay with lying, being sexually involved before I was ready, and being

OK with that, marrying a man seventeen years older to fill daddy issues, and being okay with that. Then I could tell you how I continued getting involved with other people who fed into dishonor, lust, and a whole host of other sins that were working in and through me.

But what about you? Are you seeing a pattern here? Families are pretty complicated, aren't they? Have you ever thought about the times your family members shamed someone else in the family? What about honor—do you tend to honor one another instead? Can you see where the goodness of honor has taken root in your family, too? Thank goodness, there are generational blessings that come down the family line as well!

I was recently with my best friend of over thirty-eight years, Marcelina, and we were praying together about how to minister to others out of what we've been through. She said something that just blew my mind: "You can't cast out what you have in common!"

What a profound statement! Since then, I've started realizing that for years, what I had inside me, I attracted in other people. Let me say that again—what I had in me, I attracted. Follow me here and try not to let religious thinking make you want to look away. Don't take offense— believe me, I had that religious spirit too.

I had the spirit of lust in me, so I drew that to myself from others who had that same spirit. I had the spirit of dishonor in me, which came to me through being dishonored by others or by my dishonoring others. Think about that concept for a minute. Now, think about what that looks like generationally for you and me.

Yes, Christians can be influenced by demonic spirits. I'm not talking about possession here—I'm talking about influence. I'm talking about a pulling, an uncontrollable urge, accusations you feel even when no one has said anything.

Generational sins and iniquities aren't a new concept, but Satan doesn't want us to understand them fully. You know why? Because when you finally grasp this concept, you begin to realize that you have the power to dismantle these generational patterns in your life, affecting all your generations—past, present, and even future ones. What a concept!

Now, why wouldn't Satan want us to understand this? Power. It's one of the most powerful and freeing things I've come to understand.

Do I know all the sins my ancestors ever committed? Absolutely not. There's no way to know that. However, let's examine the number of people in our family line. Just for you to be born, you needed:

- 2 parents
- 4 grandparents
- 8 great-grandparents
- 16 second great-grandparents
- 32 third great-grandparents

- 64 fourth great-grandparents
- 128 fifth great-grandparents
- 256 sixth great-grandparents
- 512 seventh great-grandparents
- 1,024 eighth great-grandparents
- 2,048 ninth great-grandparents

For you and me to be born today, we have twelve previous generations, giving us a total of 4,094 ancestors just in the last four hundred years alone! Now let's double and triple those numbers back to Eden. That's a lot of people, and people can be messy!

There's no way for us to know who did what in our families. My friend Dr. Ron Horner says, "Most of my ancestors didn't go to Sunday school." As I said, there's no way for us to know all the sins and iniquities that come from our family line, but I know Someone who does.

Thinking along those lines, what righteousness did Eve bring to the next generation? What about Adam? We know that they learned a great deal during their daily walks with the Father.

March 16, 2021, Journal Entry

The Lord had me go outside and sit. This is what He spoke:

Look at the trees. I made them, each one unique in design. Perfecting My Glory. Designed uniquely to fulfill a purpose. They show their splendor. They sing to Me. Every branch, every limb is perfected, designed exactly how I wanted. It houses beautiful things within, just like you. Like Mankind. All perfected by My design. Every color, every creed. All extensively created by My hand. Look at each person knowing they are designed by Me. Each one precious, priceless in My eyes. I count it all joy. Each is unique for My purpose, My will. All for My Glory. You think one is more unique than another? It is not so. Like any artist, each is specialized down to every detail, from every nail and hair. Count it all joy with each creation I make. Count it all sorrow with each destroyed—a Moses, an Elijah, and a Samuel I will bring. When you destroy a man, even with your words, it is against Me, their creator. Each was designed and given breath by My might, not yours. Would you have others look at and speak to and about you the way you have spoken about others?

You speak about Me when you do those things. You speak against My design, My perfection, My House (our body) created to house My spirit. My hand is upon them the same as it is upon you. Their lot is the same as your lot. Choose Me and live. Don't choose Me and die. There is no one greater except My Son. Call upon His name and I will heal the land.

Your hearts, bind them one to another. There will be no lack. It will be a strength to be reckoned with. Let no man put asunder the words I have spoken this day; I will deal with each heart accordingly. Humbleness shall be exalted. Each person you pass, pray for them. Thank Me for them, yes, even the stranger. For I will bind all of your hearts together. I will do what I have proclaimed!

Friend, isn't it amazing how God sees us? Even when we're caught up in generational patterns of dysfunction, He sees the beautiful design He created. He sees the potential for breaking cycles and starting new legacies of honor and blessing.

The journey of understanding our generational patterns isn't about shame—it's about freedom. When we can identify what's been passed down, we can choose to break the negative cycles and pass down blessings instead. We can be the generation that says, "This stops with me," and "This blessing starts with me."

Are you ready to discover what needs to be broken in your generational line? Are you prepared to step into the freedom that comes with understanding your true identity in Christ, separate from the patterns that have held your family captive?

The adventure is just beginning, and I promise you—it's worth every step of the journey.

Chapter 4:

Legal Rights

I ask a lot of questions—it's just who I am. Like, what is sin anyway? What about iniquity? Did you know those two words mean entirely different things? I didn't, and I grew up in church! Why aren't our pastors talking about these distinctions anymore? Since we covered the definitions in the last chapter, we're starting to get a clearer picture now.

Look, remember what I told you before—I'm just a regular girl asking questions. I don't have all the answers. But what I do know, I'm happy to share with you. At some point, I made a decision that changed everything. I decided to do something about what was affecting me, so it would finally stop. I drew a line in the sand and said, "It ends with me—this hard life ends with me." I love my children so much that I knew these patterns had to be broken.

Most of us know that Jesus came and died for us—that's not news. But here's what we aren't often taught: It was once and for all. What does that even mean? He came one time to die for ALL sin and iniquity, so why do we still struggle so much? We struggle because we aren't taught that Satan knows this truth, but he's found a way to use legal rights against us to keep us trapped in these cycles of consequences. After all, he is the accuser of the brethren.

Revelation 12:10

Then I heard a loud voice saying in heaven, "Now salvation, and strength, and the kingdom of our God, and the power of His Christ have come, for the accuser of our brethren, who accused them before our God day and night, has been cast down.

Hebrews 4:16

Let us then approach God's throne of grace with confidence, so that we may receive mercy and find grace to help us in our time of need. (NIV)

Want to know what that legal right is? It's the unconfessed sin—the secret sins within us and those who came before us. So technically, my great-great-great-grandparents did something they weren't even sorry for, and here I am, born years and years (and years) later, struggling to overcome something as simple as lying. Why? Why is it so hard?

Because there's a legal right that Satan is using against me. It allows demonic entities to wreak havoc in my life—

legally. But Jesus's death, burial, and resurrection provided a way for us, right? Yes! He allows us to go before the highest court—His Mercy Court—to confess these sins and iniquities on behalf of ourselves and our family line to receive justice.

We can ask to step into the Mercy Court through Jesus to receive mercy in our time of need, just like Hebrews 4:16 tells us.

Think about Daniel for a minute. He realized the seriousness of his forefathers' sins—so much so that he stood before the Lord and confessed not only his sins, but also those of his forefathers (Daniel 9:4-6). When he did that, it was done. He didn't know all the specific things they had committed, but he knew it was enough to put him and his people into slavery.

That's what's happening with you and me today. It's a form of slavery—we're living in a form of slavery to these generational patterns. You've probably heard songs about being a slave to sin, but we can indeed be free. Daniel restored honor to his generations, and we can too.

I wonder if Eve ever thought things could be restored after the fall? What about Cain?

There are lots of resources and ways to do this work of repenting on behalf of generations, renouncing, forgiving, and simply standing in the gap. Let me paint a picture for you.

Using your imagination, see yourself in a courtroom setting. You've been to court before, right? Maybe not, but you've seen it in movies. Picture that scene as you try this out. You're standing in front of a judge—not just any judge, but the highest judge in Heaven. Your counsel is beside you, and that would be Jesus. The enemy, the accuser of the brethren, is to your right.

Begin to ask the Lord, "What is it that the accuser has against me?" Listen to the Holy Spirit. Something might drop into your spirit—you might hear a word, see something, or feel a certain way. Once something has been laid on your heart, repent or forgive as the Spirit leads you.

This creates an actual legal court case before the Just Judge of Heaven. Doing this by faith, in this "court setting," is how I've been shown that the Lord removes all the loopholes the enemy has against us. Want to know why this works? It's all about forgiveness. It's also about repentance.

When you acknowledge a sin or iniquity in your life and repent of it, everything changes. You'll begin realizing that somewhere, someone in your generational line opened the door to the things that haunt you today. Agree with the adversary and then forgive yourself and your generations as well. Why not? What do you have to lose?

This key begins to unlock the chains that have bound you to certain oaths, vows, covenants, sins, and iniquities. As you stay in a place of forgiving those who hurt you or your family, Jesus can then take away ALL the enemy's ability to harm you as you willingly stand in this court of mercy. Jesus is there as your counsel against the accuser of the brethren—you know, the one who has had a legal right against you.

He doesn't have a leg to stand on anymore and can no longer be your accuser because of the blood that Jesus shed. Because of Jesus, you're able to receive your righteous verdict from a loving Father.

I won't take us down the whole road of how-tos for generational cleansing here—those resources will be in the back of this book. But for now, know that this is how and where I found my freedom.

March 26, 2021, Journal Entry

I stepped into the shower and said to the Lord that I wanted to enter into what I had been learning about Heaven being availed to us now. How could we enter into the realms of Heaven? I took a real step in the natural, by faith, and suddenly felt a woman in white linen greeting me. She was blonde. I asked if she was an angel, and she simply replied, "I am a helper." She told me her name was Tabitha, and I immediately began to question myself. However, my vision quickly opened up, and she led me to the "Halls of Recompense." I had never heard of anything like that. I didn't know what that was or what it meant. I began to hear faint music in the background, really faint. The hall didn't have any ceilings, and I realized God was there! He began pouring something on me. It was so white it almost looked solid, but it flowed like hot liquid all over me and inside of me.

Then I was led to the Glory Room by a different woman in white linen. In between all of this, I told the Lord, "Yes" to whatever He wanted. He said that some of what I will go through will be hard, but he told me my daughters would be OK. I entered the Glory Room, a vast space with gold walls.

I saw a beautiful fabric coming from the left side of the room, up the walls, and watched it cover the length of the room and up the other side of the opposite wall. I realized it was God's train that he wears. I was standing on part of it. It was soft and springy. I realized I could jump on it. Suddenly, I saw my two friends there. My one friend would run and jump on the fabric, then slide down. I could hear us all laughing with such joy. Then all of a sudden, my son was there. He was probably five years old. He was so beautiful. His hair was even beautiful. I kept telling him how beautiful he was. He told me he prayed for me all the time and that his

Father (God) had taught him how. I was holding both of his hands, tears streaming down my natural eyes.

Friend, can you imagine the freedom that comes when you realize you don't have to stay trapped in the same patterns that have held your family captive for generations? When you understand that Jesus provided a legal way for you to break free from every accusation the enemy has held against you and your family line?

This isn't just about you—this is about your children, your grandchildren, and generations you'll never even meet. When you step into that courtroom of mercy and allow Jesus to be your advocate, you're not just changing your own life. You're changing the entire trajectory of your family's future.

The beautiful thing is, God wants this freedom for you even more than you want it for yourself. He's been waiting for you to discover this truth, to step into this place of mercy, and to let Him wash away every legal right the enemy has held against you.

Are you ready to step into that courtroom? Are you ready to let Jesus be your advocate and watch Him dismantle every accusation that's been holding you back?

The door is wide open, and your loving Father is waiting.

Chapter 5:

Heavenly Encounters

Think about this for a moment—Eve had Heavenly encounters every single day before the fall. She and Adam literally walked with the Father in the cool of the day. Can you even imagine that kind of intimacy?

Genesis 3:8-10

And they heard the sound of the Lord God walking in the garden in the cool of the day, and Adam and his wife hid themselves from the presence of the Lord God among the trees of the garden.

Having experienced how Heaven reveals itself to me has given me a completely new perspective on what Eve must have gone through after that moment in the garden. To be in perfect communication with Love—His perfect love for them—and then lose that? I can't imagine how difficult life became mentally and emotionally. I say that because I can't even fathom being separated from Him the way they were, after being fully in the Trinity's presence for who knows how long.

It's only been a few years since this revelation came to me, but I've never been the same. Intimacy has been restored. Love abounds.

March 27, 2021, Journal Entry

While continuing to work on stepping into that dimensional realm of Heaven, I was met by Victoria again, who gave me a giant bag. She dropped it at my right foot. I asked what it was, and she said, "All monies lost." Another bag arrived, a see-through one, and it was filled with gold coins. They were put in my left hand. Another person in white gave me beautiful flowers for my garden. (As I am writing this 4 years later, I know this is for the garden inside of me, Eden.) Then a person, Bob, gave me a white box with a blue ribbon. I opened it, and there was a beautiful robe inside. They all said they were happy I was there. I found that curious.

Then, I saw my grandmother, GG. She was so young and beautiful. (I was extremely close to her when she was alive.) Then I saw nothing but light, moving, changing colors, moving more, and then a quick glimpse of the Throne.

My vision began looking to the left, and I saw water. I walked over and put both of my feet in. I saw angels, the second one that came to guard my daughter, as well as many others. They simply nodded and waved at me. Then I saw a very long line of people in white linen. They gave me trinkets; I am unsure what that means. One gave me "Justice that I am supposed to serve." No idea what that means.

In March of 2021, I was introduced to this incredible idea: We are Sons of God (that's a positional place, not about gender) who have the right and privilege to walk in the realms of Heaven right now. We can have encounters, seek godly wisdom, experience the Courts of Heaven, and receive incredible visions today, while we're alive and breathing.

Think about it like this—if earthly kings have children, what do those children inherit from their parents? EVERYTHING! He's our Father; we're His kids. He loves us, and what Jesus did for us has made this very thing available to us. We get the Kingdom, and we get it now. Yes, we'll go there after our physical bodies pass away, but Jesus has made this available to us right here, right now.

John 10:10

The thief does not come except to steal, and to kill, and to destroy. I have come that they may have life and that they may have it more abundantly.

John 10:10

The thief shepherd has no other agenda but to steal, kill, and he couldn't care less if he lost some sheep. I have come with the sole purpose for you to have life in its most complete form. (THE MIRROR)

Now, just like anything else, this becomes a matter of trust with the King of Kings. If you're a complete beginner and you're expecting Elijah-style encounters right off the bat, you'll probably be disappointed. This lifestyle is about intimacy and earning the right to be close to the Father's heart. You will experience Him, and it will build over time. It's the most beautiful journey I've ever been on.

My best friend of thirty-eight years, Marcelina, introduced our group—the Back Porch Girls (eight friends who met every week to pray for our families and the nation)—to this revelation in 2021. Her journey is unique, just like many of ours. She was desperately seeking answers for a family member.

Like many of us evangelicals, we wanted the next greatest move of God right this minute. We've all been there, right? Crying, interceding, rebuking, spitting, and screaming at the enemy. You know who you are! We were taught that we needed all that intensity. It was definitely for a season, but we're in a new Kingdom season now.

Her journey led us to this revelation, and wow, did it change us forever. What's so precious about this time in our lives is that all eight of us walked this revelation out together. We learned it together and continue to experience this daily.

Within a few months of discovering this, five of the eight of us were off to our first conference to learn about the Courts of Heaven. That trip sealed the deal for us. You can't take away our experiences. When you experience God, the angels, and the cloud of witnesses from and through the realms of Heaven right now while you're living and breathing, you'll never be the same.

March 30, 2021, Journal Entry

In prayer time, God put on my whole armor for me. The shield of Faith, then the helmet of salvation, the sword of the Spirit, the shoes of the preparation of the gospel, and the breastplate of righteousness. He said, "You are a warrior. I have a commission for you." (Last week, the angel said I had an assignment)

When I first entered, I was standing in a field of flowers, and I began to run my hand through them; they sounded like tinkling bells. I realized the ground was very soft, it had the texture of blood under the grass, but it wasn't blood like we think of it.

I began seeing and walking through the "Halls of Praise" that led to the "Cathedral of Praise" in the realms of Heaven. I could hear songs, and I could see rainbows in the atmosphere. I asked to enter the Courts of Heaven on behalf of my generational bloodline on my biological father's side. I brought up that I had already come here for this but had a gut feeling something was off as I received what looked like evil documents. Then the Just judge told me that the enemy had appealed the original righteous verdict. I didn't understand it at the time, so I did more repentance work and heard, "Dismissed and thrown out" and knew it was over.

I was so hungry for more of these experiences, but I had zero framework for this in my spiritual background. This was completely new territory. But isn't that what we should be walking in? The new everyday? Scripture tells us He gives us new mercies every morning.

Lamentations 3:22-23

Because of the Lord's great love, we are not consumed, for His compassions never fail. They are new every morning; Great is your faithfulness. (NIV)

Having no framework for this concept helped me in a way—I didn't have to undo spiritual limitations in my mind. I want to challenge everyone reading this book to realize this is attainable. This is His will, it's His heart to allow you to encounter Heaven, to encounter Him like you've never been able to conceive before in your spiritual journey.

This isn't spiritism, it's not occultic or false doctrine. No! This is relationship. This is you and Heaven. No one is "teaching" you, guiding you, or telling you what's happening. These are *your* personal experiences between you and the One who created you. That's why no one will ever be able to take away your experiences. It's something so special that it stays with you and fills every void you've ever had.

March 31st, 2021, Journal Entry

I stepped into the realms of Heaven through Jesus, the only way. I was met by a woman in white named Amy. She took me to the "Halls of Recompense." It was full of treasures! Everywhere, lining the walls were treasures. The Father told me to take them all. He showed me my son who was running around the room so excited that those gifts were for me! I instinctively began scooping them up and putting them inside of me. Then I saw a host of angels. They were assigned or given to me. The Father said I would fight with them! He had already adorned me with large necklaces of wisdom and knowledge, and yesterday, He dressed me in my armor. He said I was the apple of His eye. He has commissioned me.

Amy, a woman in white, gave me a scroll and I took it. I have an assignment. I am a warrior for the Kingdom. Those who are the least in the Kingdom shall be the greatest. Jesus came and took my hand as a symbol to me that he would be walking in this and through this with me! Holy Spirit reminded me that he had put his right hand on my left shoulder and had spoken, "It is time." From the Hall of Recompense and the "Registrar's office," (I dare you to look up that definition) I received these redeemed items: I wrote, "I Stephanie am here to receive cash and stocks that I am owed from, the company. Holy Spirit, Jesus Christ, and the Lord God Almighty paid for this." I was given a bag of money, and I was asked by a person in white, "Do you have the deed?"

(Deed: A legal document that is signed and delivered, especially one regarding the ownership of property or legal rights.)

I gave them the deed that appeared in my hand, the person in white took it, stamped it, and a huge pile of gifts and money appeared.

Here's something that breaks my heart to think about: Do you think God, in His mercy, ever allowed Eve or Adam to have any Heavenly encounters again after the fall? After my own taste of His Kingdom—the one that is forever—I can't imagine having that kind of intimacy and then losing it.

But here's the beautiful thing, friend—because of what Jesus did, we don't have to wonder about that anymore. We don't have to live separated from Heaven. We can walk in that garden with Him again, right here, right now. We can experience the intimacy that was lost and reclaim what was always meant to be ours.

The door to Heaven isn't closed to us. In fact, it's wide open, and our Father is waiting to walk with us in the cool of the day, just like He did with Adam and Eve. The question isn't whether this is available—it's whether we're ready to step through that door and into the most incredible adventure of our lives.

Are you ready to discover what it means to have Heaven encounters while you're still breathing? Are you ready to experience intimacy with your Creator that will change everything about how you see yourself, your life, and your future?

The garden is waiting for you to come home.

Chapter 6:

The Truth of the Matter

Genesis 3:24

So He drove out the man; and He placed cherubim at the east of the garden of Eden, and a flaming sword which turned every way, to guard the way to the tree of life.

When we read Genesis, we see that the angels Adam and Eve encountered were the ones placed at the Garden entrance with that flaming sword, making sure they could never return. It makes me wonder—had they experienced angels before the fall?

Now here's something to think about: Imagine your typical argument with your spouse or family member. Do you think Adam blamed Eve when the angels weren't there to help him anymore? Would you? You've probably thought about that, right?

Suddenly, Adam had to start tilling the ground and growing food to sustain his family. I'm betting he and Eve had plenty of help before the fall—probably had everything they could ever want or need. But what about after? Did he dishonor her, or did he take ownership of the role he played that day in the garden?

Have you ever experienced angels? I mentioned that when I was little, I saw demons all the time. But I was in my fifties before I started experiencing angels! They do say we entertain angels without even knowing it. I'm kind of sad that my spiritual senses weren't heightened enough to see angels when I was younger.

Hebrews 13:2

Do not forget to entertain strangers, for by so doing some have unwittingly entertained angels.

April 2, 2021, Journal Entry

I was introduced to many angels, and I was told, "You will send them to the nations. You have big work to do."

(Note: One of the wonderful opportunities I have the privilege of doing in this ministry is helping people learn how to co-labor with their angels.)

Do you think Eve missed the garden? Did she ever get to experience the Tree of Life? Did Adam?

Let's talk about something many people haven't recognized yet. The very first act of betrayal and dishonor happened right there in the garden. Yes, Eve was seduced, but here's the thing—Adam was standing right next to her when she ate the fruit! Why didn't he stop her? And when the Father asked what they were doing, why did Adam immediately throw her under the bus?

He took no ownership whatsoever. He acted like he had nothing to do with it, even though he was standing right beside her. He took the fruit too and then sin entered the world. I'm not man-bashing here—I'm just wanting us all to see that the very first sin after eating the apple was dishonoring that poor woman by throwing her under the bus.

Genesis 3:12

Then the man said, "The woman whom You gave to be with me, she gave me of the tree, and I ate."

If we're going to talk about generational iniquity and curses on the bloodline, this is where we can start. Dishonor has walked through every generation since then.

It's been deeply embedded in the beginning of every family line. But here's the beautiful thing—if we can do the good work of repenting and forgiving the sins our ancestors committed, all the way back to Eden, can you imagine the transformation this world could experience?

April 3, 2021, Journal Entry

I stepped into Heaven, and I was in a garden. I realized it was my own. I began to see a large wall made of beautiful stones, covered in moss and ivy, with beautiful flowers and vines everywhere. Jesus came, he told me the wall was strong like me. That it was fortified. I began to see my pets that had passed away! Jayce, Kisses, Pepper, and Kayla were all playing together, running around this garden. My son joined us. I realized my garden has grown since my very first encounter with it, so many years ago, before I ever understood any of this.

April 5th, 2021, Journal Entry

Heaven said, "I will reveal the hidden things and instruct you day and night."

April 6, 2021, Journal Entry

As I have been repenting for my sins and my generations, I received a Certificate of Completion from Heaven. It said, 'Debt Paid in Full' to the end of slavery, and I was given a 'Bond of Freedom.' I was given flowers for my garden. I realized I was sitting on a bench in the garden. I could feel the coolness and peace. Was I in the cool of the day in Heaven with the Father?

There's something incredible about freedom, friend. Having these very personal encounters showed me that the truth is, we haven't been told the whole truth from the pulpit. It's been lost even to our pastors—they're not taught this stuff in seminary!

Why wouldn't the enemy want to steal this truth from the body of Christ? It's incredibly powerful, full of authority and weight, especially when you recognize the value of removing legal rights from you and your generations. What a calling! The enemy absolutely hates these things, which is why he's kept masses of people stuck in religion instead of relationship.

Jesus wants a relationship with us, not adherence to the doctrines of men. Yes, we need some order when dealing with large groups of people, but we should never add to or take away from the gospel, especially the relational side of the gospel—the gospel of love.

Matthew 15:9

But in vain they do worship me, teaching for doctrines the commandments of men. (KJV)

April 7, 2021, Journal Entry

Jesus presented Himself to me as King. He showed me His crown. Then, it felt like I was in the third person walking through tall flowers with Him. He took me to a beautiful lake and mountain setting. Then suddenly, He put me in a box. He said I would be persecuted (for His sake). He said that he has my children, but they had to choose what's coming. He took me back to my garden, where I saw my pets again. They told me I had been a good mama.

(Note: This struck home as I am writing this four years later. This happened. I was put in a box by others, and I was indeed persecuted. Dishonor and betrayal at its highest, or so I thought.)

Friend, here's what I want you to understand from all of this: The patterns that started in the garden don't have to continue in your life. That first dishonor, that first blame-shifting, that first betrayal—it doesn't have to define your family line anymore.

When we can see the truth of what really happened in Eden—that both Adam and Eve played a part, that dishonor entered the picture immediately, that blame became the first response to crisis—we can finally address it. We can repent for it. We can break it.

And when we do that work, when we stand in the gap for our generational lines and say, "enough is enough," something beautiful happens. We get to experience the garden again. We get to walk with our Father in the cool of the day. We get to know what it feels like to be truly free.

The certificate that says "Debt Paid in Full" isn't just for me—it's available for you too. The bond of freedom isn't just my inheritance—it's yours, too. The garden isn't just a memory of what was lost—it's a present reality of what has been restored.

Are you ready to do the work? Are you ready to break the cycles that have held your family captive since Eden? Are you ready to experience the freedom that comes with all debts being paid and all legal rights being removed from the enemy's hands?

Your garden is waiting, and your Father is ready to walk with you in the cool of the day.

Chapter 7:

Changed

I can hardly begin to express how much this understanding has changed not only my life, but also the lives of everyone around me who is walking this out as well. His goodness truly extends to all of His children. His perfect will is that you experience Him too, right now, in this life, not just when we die.

Yes, we'll spend eternity in a relationship we've never experienced before. Still, Heavenly encounters with Jesus, with the Father, and even with family members who've gone before us are real and available now. Try this approach and watch as your own Heavenly encounters begin to intensify over the coming months and years. As I began to walk in this, things started to change drastically for me—both emotionally and physically—as Jesus was making all things new.

April 17, 2021, Journal Entry

So much has happened over the last two weeks, I've been completely down in my back for eight days now. This past Wednesday, April 14th, the Back Porch Girls prayed for my back. I heard, "Root of bitterness." I had already gone through and finished both books by Dr. Ron Horner, Overcoming the False Verdicts of Freemasonry *and* Freedom from Mithraism. *I do believe I addressed a lot of issues. So, on Friday, I was in the shower praying, and I asked to be allowed to step into Heaven. I saw white floors immediately. I walked to the help desk, and they walked me to a Heavenly hospital. We went into labor and delivery. While in this labor and delivery room, I saw babies being delivered. I don't know what it means just yet. Then we passed a very large window, and I saw a lot of babies swaddled, all wearing white hats.*

The person in white walking with me said we are going to the ER. I got on the table, and I was thinking I was going to get something for my back. However, Jesus came and, with a pair of tongs, pulled a black box out of the center of my body. It was small but very worn out. Then I heard that I was getting a new exoskeleton for my soul. I didn't understand the black box and assumed it was a result of some sort of sin. Then Heaven said, 'You're going to the recovery room.' When I got there, I was instructed to be in recovery in the natural for three days. Then I talked to my best friend about this encounter, and she said, "Stephanie, you know that when planes go down, the first thing they go find is the black box. Why? Because it records everything! I suddenly had a knowing that all the screaming, yelling, pain, disappointment, unforgiveness, and evil words that had ever been spoken were taken out with the removal of that black box!"

Let me be completely honest with you—I was a really bad person. I mean, really bad. My life had been this continuous mess of terrible relationships, poor decisions, deaths of hope, and constant betrayal and dishonor. I mentioned earlier that I was an angry drunk who felt abandoned by others, so I abandoned others. I was betrayed, so I betrayed. I was dishonored, so I dishonored.

Want to know a secret? Actually, you're supposed to say no because secrets are bad! They bind us! It's Satan's sick joke on humanity—holding secrets over us. Let me tell you about one of mine.

I was so sick at heart for much of my young life because of an abortion I had in my twenties. I've come to understand that this was innocent bloodshed that I was responsible for. It was murder—there's no way around it. I couldn't bear for my family to know about this. I was with the person I loved most (the father of the child) when this happened, and I truly believe that what we did by taking our child's life is what ruined our relationship. This was yet another generational iniquity that had been plaguing me.

Let me scream this from the mountaintops: Heavenly, personal encounters have been the only thing that saved my mind, my heart, and my life. Jesus coming face to face with me and whispering, "I am not your accuser"—that saved me. I truly believed I was someone who could never be used to pray for people, much less work for the kingdom. Yet He's shown me that He knows who was really behind that belief system, and He let me off the hook.

April 19, 2021, Journal Entry

One week and four days of being down with my back. Today was hard for me. That's weird for me to say since at the beginning of this, I was being taken into Heaven and to the healing hospital and told to rest for three days. I needed to stay in a recovery room for a period. It was hard because I was so discouraged because of the pain. It had even moved up into my left shoulder. I did wake up to a dream regarding a family member. This family member spoke to me in a different language, and I knew it was demonic. So, I spoke in tongues. Long story short, I lay on the floor of my den and inquired of the Lord about this dream. I realized that I had been her accuser. Where she had accused me, I had also accused her. There were a lot of tears and a lot of confessions on my part. I even saw a millstone around my own neck. After much humbleness and repentance, I asked the Lord to go after her and save her—so many, many tears.

If I can walk in the realms of Heaven and come face to face with Jesus, you can too. You see, Jesus doesn't remember my sins—the enemy does. That's why Jesus has chosen to be our counsel in Heaven. He took the judgment upon himself. The enemy—the one who comes to steal, kill, and destroy—has blinded all of us to the truth that it is finished. It's the enemy who accuses us day and night, dredging up the sins of the past that are in our very blood. That's why generational cleansing is so necessary.

April 22, 2021, Journal Entry

Whoa. Imagine what I thought when I looked down and re-read this encounter. I knew I could trust it because deceit has no place in Heaven. It explained the pain. If you want real answers for your life, Step in. If you want the nagging questions to be answered, Heaven is waiting.

Two and a half years after writing that journal entry, I was at a Daniel Adams conference in my hometown. All of us went down to the front to be prayed for, and as he walked by me, he stopped, put his hand above me, and said, "You have a rage deep inside of you." Then he just walked off! I thought to myself, "What? Are you just going to leave me like this?"

Rage is on most generational lines, but I didn't even recognize it in myself. I knew I had a quick temper, and I knew I could get so angry that I'd get a headache. But I didn't realize I needed Jesus to step into my timeline and heal me of what had happened to me as a child.

April 25, 2021, Journal Entry

I heard Jesus say as he handed me a scroll, "I am giving you back the lost, the stolen. I am turning back time and seasons for you and your family. You fought for it. I have designed you to lead. Follow me. Your instructions are to go, to show, to see. I've undone the done in your time. There is more to come. See this, it's a time and space in which I don't work, but I can move, shift, and "suddenlies" will take place. It has been moved or replaced. The blood is applied. You are wed to me. You requested it. It is. The enemy is silenced. The truth is near of what others will see. Be silent. Hear."

What's crazy is, it's me He's speaking to! Little old me! At the beginning of all this, I couldn't understand why He would want me. But He bought me. He paid for me. He wants me. And friend, He wants you too. It doesn't matter what you've done. I haven't even scratched the surface of what I've done, but that doesn't matter to Him. He doesn't care what you or I have done. He sees me as innocent, and He sees you as innocent too.

May 11, 2021, Journal Entry

Today, I stepped into Heaven and requested my books and records. I presented them to the Father. I also handed him a key that I knew I had in my hand. He gave me a giant page with an A+. I laughed with Him. He looked at my books. Then Jesus came up, and I had a knowing that I was to ask for the thing in His pocket. Jesus gave it to me, and I gave it to the Father. It turned into a hologram of a child, very small, very young. He told me to take her, so I did. She wrapped her little arms around my neck and tucked her head under my chin. She was so little and so precious. I asked the Father who she was. He

said, "She is you. She is love that had been taken."
Oh, I held her for a long time.

Then He handed me a scroll and told me to go to the "Halls of Recompense." There was a guard at the gate. I gave him the scroll, he opened it, read it and the doors opened. It was a massive room, like a castle. It was "old" in the sense that it was ancient. There was a large table with a note on it, a candelabra and a sword. I was told to get the note. I opened it and it said "Accepted." The Lord told me to wear it like a badge. I put it on then I picked up the candelabra, it had multiple flames.

I had a knowing to put it inside of me. I picked up the sword. It was long and sharp. I could see my reflection when I held it up to my face. I put it inside of me. Then there was a footstool. I asked what it was. The Father said I would use it to rest, to sit at his feet. The world is His footstool. This was mine to rest on in front of Him. I put it inside of me. He gave me Matthew 16:19, and I read it.

Matthew 16:19

I will give you the keys of the kingdom realm to forbid on earth that which is forbidden in Heaven and to release on earth that which is released in Heaven. (TPT)

This period in my life was when the realms of Heaven and the Courts of Heaven really unfolded for me. Spiritually, all of Heaven was being opened up in a way that's only understood through experience. Until you taste it—and you can—there are no proper words to describe it.

This isn't some lofty, pie-in-the-sky, unattainable religious experience. Until you have the very personal encounters created just for you, it's hard to comprehend. My experiences are unique to me, and yours will be unique to you.

I started following Dr. Ron Horner and LifeSpring International Ministries even more intensely than before. I was so hungry for His Word (the Father's), His truths, and His love through this prayer approach that I began listening to every video, reading every book, and attending every free Zoom I could. I did this because I realized this ministry actually teaches you how to do this for yourself— how to begin receiving intimate revelation with your Creator.

When you receive a word from Jesus himself in your heart, you know that you know that you know it's real. Your heart can't justify a word like that or tell you that someone might have gotten it wrong by speaking over you. No—you receive words from a loving, accepting, joyful Creator who WANTS to meet with you daily!

Confirmations: The Father and all of Heaven loves to confirm things they're teaching us. On May 11th, 2021, I received a prophetic word from Aprile Osborne, author of *Seeing Behind Enemy Lines: Exposing and Overcoming Satan's Strategies Against Your Life*. This forever changed me as I could see the Father move upon my life with each word she spoke. Here's the word she released over me:

May 11, 2021, Prophetic Word

I saw, sitting on your nightstand, a book, like a journal. I don't think it is there right now, but it was really dusty, and it said on it, "Dreams." The Lord began to blow on it. I could see him blowing on your dream book, and He wanted me to tell you, the Holy Spirit wants you to know that He wants you to dream again. You are carrying a sound inside of you that unlocks regions. There is something about you that is very authoritative, and that is why the enemy has been after your backbone. The Lord began to speak to me about your backbone. Because the enemy is very afraid of you, he has bullied you for a very long time because of the sound that you are carrying.

What most people don't know is that God created the earth, He put a sound in every single region, and I can prove it. The Bible says that if we don't cry out, the rocks will cry out and worship

Him. In every region, there is a sound in the rocks that also unlocks a portal to Heaven, bringing a move of God and the authority of Heaven into that region. You carry the authority to hear that sound in every region that you go to. The enemy has tried to bully you and muzzle you, and he came after your backbone because he doesn't want you to stand to release this sound that you carry. I don't know if you are a worship leader, a singer, or a writer, but you have the authority to write poetically. I don't know how you release it—I hear it by a sound, like a realm of Heaven. When I see you, I can hear this angelic unlocking around you like "singing" of this. I wish you could hear it because it is super loud in my ear, but you have such an authority. I wanted to really encourage you to pull out your journal again and begin to write with Him, and dream with Him again. He wants you to sit down with Him and just dream with Him again. I can see you years ago. You were a big, big dreamer. The Lord wants you to dream like that again, like a child, to come back and sit on His lap and dream. So, I am going to pray over you.

Thank you, Father, for Stephanie. I thank you for this assignment that you have upon her life, God. I thank you, Holy Spirit, for this supernatural healing that you are doing in her body, even in Relationships. There have been some relationships around you that have been painful. Thank you, Holy

Spirit, that you are going to bring healing to that right now, in Jesus' name. I thank you, Father, for restoration in her life. Thank you, Father, for this unlocking in her voice right now in the name of Jesus. Every demonic spirit of death that would come against you, come against your voice, come against your body, come against your mind and emotions, I bind that off of you NOW in Jesus' name. I unloose the sounds of Heaven. I unlock your ears now, I unlock your mind, and your dream life to come alive again. To sit back in the eyes of the one who created you. To come sit back and lock eyes with Him, dream with Him, that you would feel the wooing of the Holy Spirit waking you up early in the morning to dine and have coffee and sit with Him, dream, and just begin to write again poetically. To hear the rhythm of Heaven again. I unlock that around her in Jesus' name. And every voice that would come and speak death over her, I bind the plan of the enemy now, in Jesus' name. I thank you, God, for transitioning her to be around the right people who give her the right place, who see the call of God, and who pull the call of God out of her, in Jesus' name. I thank you, God, for alignment in her relationships and that God strengthen them.

Take your place as daughter, take your place as authority. I thank God for the transition to transition quickly in this season, in Jesus' name. I thank you,

Father, that you began to speak in her life like never before, in this season, in Jesus' name. I thank you, Holy Spirit, for that.

Friend, I was experiencing what Adam and Eve experienced in their day-to-day walk with the Father. I was meeting Him in the cool of the day. My Eden was being restored. As I honored Him, He honored my walk with Him, taking me deeper and deeper.

This is available to you too. The same restoration, the same encounters, the same intimacy. Your Eden can be restored. Your relationship with the Father can be everything it was meant to be from the very beginning.

The question isn't whether God wants this for you—He absolutely does. The question is whether you're ready to step into the reality that Heaven is closer than you think, and your loving Father is waiting to meet with you in the cool of the day, just like He always intended.

Chapter 8:

Back to the Beginning

I meant it when I said I had been a bad person. But I didn't start out that way. Our family was actually pretty tight-knit. We had a loving family, and then my grandmother moved in with us, which became my absolute favorite time in my life. We were at church Sunday morning, Sunday night, Wednesday night, and any other time the doors were open. I loved Jesus so much. I used to love going to bed just talking to Him.

I remember our church was always teaching and preaching about Jesus coming back—literally any day— which made quite an impression on someone who wanted to actually live out her life. As I lay in bed at night, I would pray that I'd get a chance to marry and have children. I recall crying a lot during those times, not because of pain, but because of pure joy. I could feel His love so deeply. I was so young.

Then one night, I had a dream. This would have been somewhere between fourth and sixth grade—I remember because of where we were living at the time.

I sat straight up in bed, waking up with a sensation I had never experienced before. I had experienced something in this dream so real that I couldn't stop thinking about it for years—yes, years. I dreamt of being in love, and I saw this person in my dream so clearly that it drove me to look for him in real life. There was a passion in my dream that I had never felt. I had never even kissed anyone before, but in this dream, I did. This dream drove me to that boy-crazy state pretty quickly.

I believe this was a dream sent by the enemy. It was full of the wrong kind of passions, and it began pulling me away from dreaming with God to dreaming about boys and longing for that desire I felt in the dream.

Some might say this is normal for girls my age. But I would say the enemy used my family's generational iniquities and sins to try and secure my future. Through understanding how much Satan hates us—his mission being to steal, kill, and destroy—I can see how this worked. Because this lust was deep inside me, this seeking after worldly pleasures, it led to the stealing of my identity in Christ, the killing of my innocence, and, in a sense, the full destruction of my life. I became everything I had never been before. I sought out that dream feeling. I wanted to feel it again. I looked in so many places and lost myself in the process.

My journey of self-discovery, boy discovery, and world discovery completely overcame me when I was fourteen. This boy I met taught me things no one should have been taught at my age. He was older than me, but he was the church secretary's son, so it was supposed to be okay. But it wasn't. I lost myself.

The games boys played at that age absolutely ripped my heart apart. I lost a ton of weight and didn't even have the energy to speak. I remember it took so much effort just to talk loud enough for people around me to hear me. I was deeply depressed as these mind games got worse. I can't blame him—he was just a high school kid. But I felt so lost, so far from God. I believed the lie that I could never have what I'd had before with Jesus.

I spent the next few years moving further and further away from innocence and peace. I allowed others to use me just so I could feel something. I played the part at church and in front of my family, but I was hurting so badly. I knew what I was doing was wrong, but I justified it. I didn't do drugs. I drank, but not a lot. This was my way to feel pretty, feel loved, feel accepted. It was a way to feel something.

What I used to experience with Jesus was gone, and I just wanted to feel again. Listen, Jesus didn't go anywhere—I did. He was patiently waiting for me.

I met another boy when I was nineteen, and I became pregnant. I couldn't bear to think of the judgment my family would place on me or what people in my church would say. You see, I still went to church. I still played the part. So, I decided the best thing for everyone involved was if I had an abortion.

I do want to add here that I spoke to a friend from school about this, and she tried to talk me out of it. I respect her to this day. Jamie, thank you.

Looking back now, I can say I didn't see it as killing my child. I was so blinded by fear and judgment that all I wanted was a way out. I cried that day. I cried through the entire procedure. Something happened to me while I lay on that cold table—I shed innocent blood. I had no idea about the trauma and consequences that lay before me. I had no idea I had played right into the devil's hands.

There are four things God hates: Profane worship, moving boundary stones, stealing wages, and innocent bloodshed. These are based on the story of Jezebel, Ahab, and Naboth's vineyard.

I married that boy who would have been the father to our child, but it didn't last. I loved him so much, and I truly believe that what I did killed our relationship.

Then one day, a few years later, I was lying in a tanning bed after working out at the gym, and wouldn't you know it—Jesus walked into that room just like He had when I was four years old. His love filled the entire room. He told me that what I had done was very wrong. Oh, I cried in that tanning bed. But He didn't make me feel guilty or ashamed. He didn't yell "YOU'RE WRONG!" No, I could feel His broken heart. I could feel His pain for me because of the open door I'd created in my life for the enemy to hurt me.

I repented in that very moment, and He healed my heart, one that I didn't even know was broken. Here's what's crazy: In the midst of my sin, He still came. I wasn't living right during that time, and yet He still came for me. Thank you, Jesus. You always come for us, even and especially when we don't deserve it.

A few years later, I met the man who became the father of my children. He had this fatherly way about him that made me feel safe. That would be because he was seventeen years older than I. Boy, was I wrong about feeling safe. Don't get me wrong—he loved me and our kids, but he was fighting his own demons. Alcoholism and drug abuse are no joke. I had zero clue what I was dealing with; all I knew was that it felt like hell. His struggles were truly from generational iniquity and huge secret sins that came down the family line.

God used that relationship with their father to bring me back to Him, back to Jesus. When you're living a nightmare, you will look up—I promise you that. When you're hungry, you'll look up. When you don't have peace, you'll look up. When you don't have gas in your car, you'll look up. And when you're in fear for your life, you'll definitely look up.

I could write a whole other book about the goodness of God during those times—miracle after miracle. I'll tell you just two.

One evening, I put my sweet girl in the backseat, and we were off to a Wednesday night prayer group. There was a new speaker, and he was teaching on covenant. I had never heard that word used in the context he was using that particular night, but it changed something inside me forever.

He spoke about how, in the West, we often don't understand the concept of covenant. We don't keep our word. We come in and out of relationships with others flippantly and don't bind our promises to them in a covenantal way.

When we get into any sexual relationship with someone, it creates a covenant in the spirit. I didn't know that. I probably would have been more mindful instead of carelessly creating bad covenants during those younger years.

Did you know that in places like Israel and other nations around it, their word is their bond unto death? Can you imagine? Unto death! I was thinking, "You're absolutely right—we don't get it." The teacher that night said that God never breaks His covenants, no matter what.

I became so convicted about this and grieved in my spirit, knowing I had broken covenant with others and with God.

Bound in Chains

After the service, I got in the car with my daughter and began the thirty-minute drive back home. I started weeping and crying out to God, begging Him to forgive me. Then something happened. The only way I can describe it is that I was taken into the spirit.

I found myself in this purplish-black dimension, suspended in the air with chains around my body. I had big chains, small chains, long chains, and short ones. They bound every part of my body. I heard the Lord say, "Name them." I knew He was talking about every sexual partner I'd ever had. I knew it was about every covenant with Him I had broken.

As I began speaking, chain after chain after chain began to fall. I would be weeping and speaking, and another chain would fall. I could feel His love for me, and I felt a sense of freedom. I came to in the garage of my home. I have no idea how I drove there; my sweet girl was fast asleep in the back. I knew I would never be the same.

The next day, while still in a state of bliss, I was shocked to suddenly see my husband stumble across the backyard in a drunken stupor. I couldn't believe it. It was only ten in the morning! How could he be drunk already?

Besides, I had just seen him, and he seemed fine! We didn't have a fence in our backyard, and our property bordered a field. I just knew our neighbors could see this. He kept falling, getting back up, and stumbling around the backyard. I was so humiliated and incredibly scared.

I became so angry. I felt an anger deep within me as my mind began remembering the words spoken the night before. Covenant. I looked up and began yelling and screaming at the top of my lungs to God. Then I did the thing I believed you should never do—I shook my fist at God and said, "You want me to be in covenant with this man, Your son? He's a total drunk! He's neglecting his duties as my husband and her father!

I tell you what—You want me to be with him? Then give it to me! Give me the ability to love, because I no longer love him. I have no respect for him, and I want to run. If You want me to love him, then give it to me!"

I was panting so hard after that rant. I was hot and sweaty and deeply out of breath because I had been screaming at the top of my lungs. Suddenly, these little flickers of light began to fill the room. The way I like to describe it is like when the fairy godmother shows up for Cinderella—the first thing we see is that little twinkling of lights. That's what I saw.

Then I felt something thick begin to pour over my head. It was so tangible that I was trying to wipe it from my forehead and my eyes. I kept thinking, "I shook my fist at God, I'm about to die.

But let me tell you, by the time this thick substance came to my feet, all I wanted to do was run outside, put my husband's head in my lap, and love on him. Not love him like a wife loves—love him like Jesus loves. Every time I wanted to leave after that moment, I felt it. I felt that thick oil and tingling until the day the Father released me to leave.

I've come to understand that what I felt was the anointing. The Father met me that day, in my need, in my husband's need. I challenged Him, and He, my Father, met me there. When you think you can't, He can.

Look at this second story from my journal entry from 1996:

Journal Entry from 1996

I had an open vision as I was waking up this morning. I realized I was standing in a small garden. There was a white picket fence with beautiful flowers everywhere. I could tell it was a young garden, but beautiful. There was such a bright light in front of me, like you see when the sun is first setting—it blinded me a bit. I could see that there was a trellis entry into this garden with a curved top. In the distance, I could see the outline of a man approaching. I began to feel this intense power in my belly that grew the closer this figure got. I realized this ball of power grew larger and encompassed my insides as the man came closer.

I kept thinking, this must be Jesus. I felt a love so pure; I have never tangibly felt that since. He entered the gate, and it was my biological father, Bruce. He died when I was 12, but I hadn't seen him since I was 2. He told me wonderful things that day. I don't remember them all, but two things I do remember: He told me that when he was alive, he didn't know what he was doing and how profoundly sorry he was for abandoning me. He told me he loved me so much, and then he told me this: "I see your son every day and we play together. He is remarkable."

Here I was, having this open vision in the middle of my life, living with an alcoholic while experiencing love from Heaven for a broken man. I had no idea that years later, while watching the movie The Shack, I would get to relive that moment regarding my biological father exactly as the movie captured it so beautifully. The moment in the movie when he saw his dad coming toward him in the field, they spoke, and his dad told him he was so sorry; he was then emotionally healed. Something healed inside me that day. Something changed.

God kept showing up for me. No matter what I did, He just kept showing up. I lived a very hard ten years with my husband, but I wouldn't take one day away. I lived an extraordinary life with God during that time.

My husband even quit drinking for a short time, and when he did, we began having a Christian small group in our home. It started with a friend asking to pray for a missionary friend of his, and over a year, it grew to include ninety people who came from everywhere. He used us. He used two very broken people—He used us to be with other broken people. All we wanted was to worship and love Jesus. It was a remarkable time. I had no idea it was preparing me for my future.

Although honor had been broken and restored, broken and restored, broken and restored by myself and others, Jesus kept honoring me. Even though I wasn't "worthy" of honor by my King, He chose to show me what honor feels and looks like. I was getting little glimpses along the way.

What you honor, you have the benefit of. What you dishonor, you no longer have the benefit of.

Friend, if you're reading this and recognizing pieces of your own story—the searching, the mistakes, the broken covenants, the desperate moments when you finally look up—please know that Jesus is still showing up. He's still meeting people in tanning beds and backyard moments of desperation. He's still pouring out His anointing on people who shake their fists at Him in honest frustration.

Your past doesn't disqualify you from His love. Your mistakes don't make you unreachable. He's been waiting patiently for you, just like He waited for me. And when you're ready to let Him break those chains and pour out His love, you'll discover what I discovered—that His goodness really does show up in the midst of our mess, and His love really can transform even the most broken places of our hearts.

Chapter 9:

A Southern Baptist Walks Into Heaven

Just like many of you, I come from a "Christian" background—Baptist, to be exact. But honestly? That phrase just doesn't cut it for me anymore. We "Christians" have done a pretty terrible job of representing anything that actually resembles the Kingdom of Heaven. Let's be real—we've failed big time. And that includes pastors and clergy, too. But why?

I'll tell you why: Religion. Ugh, it's honestly the worst. It's the ugliest, most demonic, disgusting thing ever. What a joke we've become! We sit on our high horses, tootling around, looking down on other people while we break every single promise to God we've ever made.

So what do we do about it? You and I and the whole world know we're flunking this test in a significant way. Now here's the lie we've been fed: That God the Father, Jesus, and Holy Spirit are up there wringing their hands because we won't change, or worse—that they don't care and are ready to bop us on the head for all the sinning we've done.

When I tell you I nearly fell off my rocker when I realized that They—the Trinity—are NOT accusing us! THEY KNOW! They know WHO is doing this to us, through us, in us, and on us! They know we don't stand a chance because the sins and iniquities on our generational lines are just too much to overcome, and it's the devil doing it anyway!

The other lie is that there's nothing that can be done about it. That we're just too far gone, there's been too much damage, we're just like our granddaddy.... These are all lies, friend.

Jesus paid for and was part of creating justice for us. He, the Holy Spirit, and the Father actually rejoice over the mercy seat! The price Jesus paid has allowed the Courts to be opened, and there's a righteous verdict waiting with bated breath for us to walk in and plead guilty by agreeing with our adversary.

Why would we do that? Because not all of our grandparents went to Sunday school. Not all of our people did good things. In fact, someone in our family line has likely committed nearly every sin imaginable. Thankfully, Ecclesiastes tells us there's no new sin under the sun. Even more thankfully, Jesus died for every sin ever committed...under the sun. Whew!

We've asked a lot of questions about Eve, but what about the Father? He loved Adam and Eve so much that He met with them every single day. Can you imagine the heartbreak and loss of relationship the Father experienced when they sinned? This is precisely why He sent Jesus.

The Father and Jesus desire us. Did you read that correctly? They desire us. Why wouldn't They have a way for us to come home while we're still living? They do have a way. This is how a Southern Baptist ended up in Heaven while she's still alive.

One of the most fascinating and profound books I've ever read was required reading when I studied the Courts of Heaven with LifeSpring International Ministries. It's called *Treasures of Darkness, Volume 2* by Joseph C. Sturgeon. It's the real-life encounters of a man with many great saints from the Bible. He pressed into prayer, and the Father gave him encounter after encounter with the likes of Moses, Gideon, David, and even Samson.

I wanted that. I wanted everything Heaven had available because I knew it was better than what I was experiencing in life. To have truth, love, and acceptance given to you daily in Heavenly encounters? You'd be crazy not to want that. But religion has told us we can't have it. (I told you religion is the worst.)

Why don't we do a better job of being the sons and daughters we're made to be and stand against that ancient spirit? Why would you deny yourself something this beautiful? The Father isn't denying you. Jesus died for you to have this kind of intimacy. Intimacy is the way.

Oh, and by the way, let me remind you again—neither Jesus nor the Father is your accuser. We do have an accuser, but it isn't them.

Friend, if you've been told that Heavenly encounters are only for super-spiritual people or that you have to wait until you die to experience Heaven, I'm here to tell you that's just not true. If a messed-up Southern Baptist like me can walk into Heaven while still breathing, so can you.

The door is open. The invitation is extended. Your Father is waiting to meet with you in ways that will blow your mind and heal your heart. The only question is: Are you ready to step through that door and discover what intimacy with your Creator looks like?

Because I promise you, it's better than anything religion ever offered you.

Chapter 10:
Perception is Everything

Have you ever wondered how you actually communicate with God? I mean, really communicate—not just throw up prayers and hope for the best? Let's start with how you communicate with people first, because there's a beautiful connection here.

I mentioned before that I'm a visual learner. People need to paint me a picture when they're talking to me, or I'll get completely lost. I typically ask for tons of details, and honestly, I give way too many details back!

A wonderful friend who counseled me and my daughters' father gave us this incredible gift of understanding how we perceive and hear from God. He told us he was asking the Lord about how people communicate, and the Father simplified it for him beautifully.

Means of Communication

He said, "I made people to communicate in many different ways, but an easy way to teach this is understanding seeing, hearing, feeling, and thinking."

We all have all of these in our communication toolkit. But here's the thing—we each have one main "door," one primary access point. For instance, I see pictures. When God speaks to me, it's like watching a movie unfold in my mind. My best friend is a thinker—a word or two will just drop into her spirit, and she'll have this deep "knowing" about something.

We're surrounded by friends who are feelers. When they walk into a room, they immediately feel everyone else's emotions. They have incredibly strong emotions themselves and can even sense the Father's emotions as well. Then there are the hearers—not only do they hear from the Lord clearly, but they're amazing communicators. And yes, they're usually the most long-winded of us all!

Now, we can operate through all of these, but as we grow in this relationship, these perceptions become stronger and stronger. I can step into Heaven now and actually smell the fresh aroma of baked bread as I'm being seated at the table prepared for me in the presence of my enemies!

How do you perceive?

So, how do you perceive? Figure that out, and your prayer life will absolutely accelerate!

Let me tell you a story that perfectly illustrates this. Four people working at the same job were all late and got called into HR. They all lived in the same neighborhood and all got stuck in the same traffic jam from a bad wreck. Here's how each of them explained it to the HR director:

Thinker: "I got stuck in a traffic jam from a wreck on Highway 5. Can I go to work now?"

Seer: "I saw the worst wreck ever! There were five cars, nineteen police officers, six EMS vehicles, and two fire trucks! There was blood EVERYWHERE! You wouldn't believe the mangled mess of bodies and traffic..." (continues to paint a very vivid picture of the carnage).

Feeler: "I can't get over that horrible wreck today. I was so traumatized by this, I think I need a minute before going back to work. I could feel the sadness of the police officers and others working the scene. My heart is aching for all of them."

Hearer: "Well, I was running late for work today and realized Tim was too, as he passed me just a few minutes before I got to my car. But guess what—as soon as I sat down, I spilled coffee all over me and had to go back in to change shirts. Anyway, I was thinking what a lovely day it was when I began to see the traffic slowing down. Man, there were people honking and acting crazy. Then I realized there was a wreck. I rolled down my window to hear the conversations and..." (on and on and on).

Does this sound like you? Which one fits you best? Once you figure it out, ask the Father, "What do you have to say to me today?" and perceive from your main "door." Then let the fun begin!

Did you know that Jesus has redeemed our imagination? He absolutely has! Who do you think gave us our imaginations in the first place? Jesus said we would have things greater than our imagination could even think of! Let Heaven take your imagination and open up His Kingdom to you.

You'll hear words you've never heard before or that aren't part of your normal vocabulary. You'll actually have to look up words and their meanings! I love that! It's a beautiful reminder that Heaven is speaking, not me.

Trust them. They love you and will never steer you wrong. Remember this: when you ask to step into Heaven through Jesus, no devil or demon is welcome there. It's the safest place that has ever existed.

(There's a lot more on this at ronhorner.com/blogs)

Chapter 11:
What's Stopping Us?

Many people have discovered the Courts of Heaven and experienced incredible breakthroughs—righteous verdicts, miracles, prayers that went unanswered for years, suddenly being answered in minutes or days, and the truest freedom you can imagine. Freedom from anxiety, depression, suicidal thoughts, addictions, troubled children, broken marriages, broken lives, and families.

But sometimes people have trouble receiving a righteous verdict at all. Let me be clear—it's not that the Father is up there like the Soup Nazi from Seinfeld saying, "No justice for you!" Absolutely not! When you don't get an answer, it just means there's more work to be done.

Heaven wants your freedom more than you do. That's the truth! You don't even know what freedoms you're missing, much less what you actually need. So listen, I always finish my prayers with, "May I have my righteous verdicts or further counsel." Inviting the Seven Spirits of God is something I make a point of doing all the time. I know I need all the help I can get, so why not bring in the big guns?

After working with hundreds of people, I've discovered the hindrance is always unforgiveness or unrepentance. Let me tell you a truth through a personal story. Hold on, because this one is tough.

A family friend came to me to share something that had happened to someone we both loved very much. My friend was able to tell me that our beloved friend had been horribly abused by someone else we knew. This grieved us both, and I, being a visual person, could not get the images out of my head.

I lay on the floor begging God to help this friend we loved and also to help me with my mental agony. I kept saying "I forgive," but it wasn't landing in my heart at all. I kept begging God to take the pain away.

I had just begun my journey with LifeSpring, learning about the Courts of Heaven. I lay on that floor for weeks begging God to take the images from me. I begged Him for answers about how I was supposed to forgive this man who stole our friend's innocence and abused them. One day, He answered me.

March 2021 Journal Entry:

Father, please take these images from my mind and help me to understand. I know I have to forgive this person, but how do I experience and feel this? How can this pain be gone? I have said I forgive this abuser, but the pain is still here! Please help me! Please save me! Please save us all from this nightmare!

Father said, "I will show you."

He opened up the scene to a courtroom in Heaven. I saw myself standing before the Just Judge, Jesus beside me, this abuser and the enemy being led in to my right. The Father began to speak. He said, "What happened is egregious in nature. In the natural, you have every right to be angry. In the natural, you have every right to hate this person, and in the natural, you have every right to want harm to come to this person. But you are not called to live in the natural. I have called you to be a peculiar people. I will let you feel all of those things if you want. I will even bless you, even though it isn't My best for you. I will allow you to hate the abuser.

"However, you have to leave this side of the courtroom where Jesus is standing and walk over to the other side of the courtroom where the enemy is. You must slip your hand in his because, if you

choose to feel those ways, you have become and are an accuser of the brethren. You must slip your hand in his because of your agreement with him to be this abuser's accuser. I will still bless you, but know this: the door to you will be open to the enemy. He will have a legal right. Not only that, but you will not have any peace of mind, these images will be allowed to come, and the friend you love will still be affected as well. The door is open. You choose. Will you let vengeance be Mine, or do you want it for yourself? I give you free will. I love this abuser that did this. I created him. I am saddened by what happened, but let me show you something."

He summoned two angels to go to this abuser and pull these demons out of him, standing them next to him in court. The Father said, "You wrestle not with flesh and blood but with principalities, powers, and rulers of darkness in wicked places."[1] He pointed to the demons and said, "That is who did this. Not the man, but the spirits IN him." Then the Father turned my attention to the man. I began to see him with a millstone around his neck. He looked horrible, scared, and so tired. The Father allowed me to see his own abuse as a boy. I began to weep. I was overwhelmed with the Father's love, and I

---

[1] Ephesians 6:12

began to ask Jesus to forgive this abuser, and I
began to ask for mercy for him.

You see, I began to feel the love in that courtroom—compassion and love from the Father, flowing into me and toward that abuser. I knew there wasn't anything I could ever do to dish out the kind of punishment he deserved, but I could receive love right there, right then, and extend it to him.

I forgave him that day. I was able to get off the floor and never had to return to that place of torment. I'm no longer tortured with the images of what happened to my beautiful friend. The sting is gone. I know the Father is working on that man's heart. It's between them now. I am free.

Chapter 12:
Coming Home

Many of us know the feeling of coming home—that sense of safety, belonging, and peace. Most people have experienced a safe place at some point, but there are some who never have. This chapter is especially for you.

The only true healer of deep wounds wants to walk with you on the streets of gold right now. He wants to take you by the hand and step with you onto the crystal sea right now. He wants to teach you about the splendor of Heaven's glorious forests right now. He wants you to meet and learn from Moses, Samuel, Paul, Mary, and so many others. Their destinies are still alive and active!

He's calling us back to Eden. The garden is in us. When we took Him as our Savior, He came INSIDE of us. We live and move and have our being in Him. He is in us, we are in Him, and we are in the Father. Eden is restored.

I am Eve. You are Eve. Listen, if men are going to be the bride of Christ, they can be Eve restored, too. I am no one special, yet I am His. That makes me something incredibly special. You are, too.

Something the Father told me recently has stayed with me. He said, "When you stood before Me in innocence, from where I created you out of Myself, I put something so special in you that only you can bring from the Kingdom of Heaven to earth."

I realized that what we've been praying—"Your Kingdom come, Your will be done on earth as it is in Heaven"—is actually true and attainable. I can now say, "Father, pull out of me what You placed in me, my destiny, and help me to bring Your will to earth from the Kingdom of Heaven."

He placed something in you that only you can bring to the earth from His Kingdom. You are so special, so unique, that if you die without completing your mission, your destiny, it will die with you. No one who lived before you and no one who will ever live after you can bring into the earth what He has put as gifts, destinies, territories, callings into you. Only you can do that.

Why do you think the enemy has been after you so hard? He's terrified of this knowledge coming to the sons and daughters (that's a positional place, not about gender). We are meant to rise up. The earth is groaning for us to realize who we are in Him.

Come on, Eves—let's do this! He has restored honor. Let's BE honor. Let's lend honor. Let's extend honor. Because truly, what you honor, you have the benefit of.

Friend, you're not reading this by accident. Your journey back to Eden, your discovery of who you really are, your unique calling that only you can fulfill—it's all waiting for you. The garden isn't just a memory; it's your present reality.

Your Father is calling you home, not someday, but today. Are you ready to step into the fullness of who He created you to be?

Conclusion:

Your Journey Home

Friend, we've traveled quite a journey together, haven't we? From the Garden of Eden to the Courts of Heaven, from generational bondage to supernatural freedom, from religious limitations to intimate encounters with our Creator. As we close this book, I want you to know that your journey is just beginning.

If you have read this far and haven't surrendered your life to Jesus, pause right now and simply say, "Jesus, I need your mercy. I've sinned and I'm sorry. I surrender to you now."

Coming Home to Truth

When I first started asking questions about Eve, I had no idea where those questions would lead me. I thought I was just wondering about a woman who made a terrible mistake in a garden thousands of years ago. But what I discovered was that Eve's story is our story. Her fall, her shame, her separation from intimacy with God—it's the human condition we've all inherited.

But here's the beautiful truth I want you to take with you: **what was lost in the garden can be restored in your life today.**

The Key Revelations

Let me remind you of the most important discoveries we've made together:

Generational Patterns Are Real—But Breakable:

Those cycles of dishonor, addiction, broken relationships, and destructive patterns that have followed your family line? They're not your destiny. They're legal rights the enemy has been using against you, but Jesus paid the price to break every chain. You can be the generation that says "enough is enough" and breaks the cycle for good.

You Have Legal Standing in Heaven's Courts:

This isn't just poetic language—it's spiritual reality. When you step into the Courts of Heaven through Jesus as your advocate, you can present cases against the accusations that have held your family captive. You can receive righteous verdicts that dismantle every legal right the enemy has claimed against you.

Heavenly Encounters Are Your Inheritance:

You don't have to wait until you die to experience Heaven. You don't have to be super-spiritual or perfect. Intimacy with your Creator, encounters with Jesus, meetings with loved ones who've gone before you—these aren't reserved for special people. They're your birthright as a son or daughter of the King.

Secrets Lose Their Power When Exposed:

Every family secret, every hidden shame, every generational sin loses its power when brought into the light. The very things the enemy has used to torment you become powerless when you're willing to agree with your adversary, repent, and receive forgiveness.

God Is Not Your Accuser:

This might be the most life-changing revelation of all. The Trinity—Father, Son, and Holy Spirit—are not up there shaking their heads at you in disappointment. They know exactly who your real enemy is, and they've provided everything you need to defeat him. They're not your judges; they're your advocates, your defenders, your loving family.

The Practical Path Forward

So, where do you go from here? How do you apply what we've learned together?

Start with Honesty:

Look at the patterns in your family line. What keeps showing up generation after generation? Financial struggles? Broken marriages? Addiction? Mental health issues? Sexual sin? Violence? Don't be afraid to see it clearly—you can't break what you won't acknowledge.

Step into the Courts:

Using your imagination, picture yourself in a heavenly courtroom. Jesus is your advocate, the Father is the just Judge, and yes, your accuser is there too. But now you have the tools to dismantle his case against you. Repent on behalf of your generations, forgive those who've hurt you, and watch legal rights crumble.

Pursue Intimacy Over Religion:

Stop settling for religious routine when intimate relationship is available. Press into those quiet moments with God. Step through Jesus into heavenly dimensions. Ask for encounters, expect to hear His voice, anticipate meeting Him in ways that will transform your understanding of who He is and who you are.

Break the Silence:

Stop keeping family secrets. Stop carrying shame alone. The enemy's power is in the darkness—bring everything into the light. Find safe people to share your story with. Get the support you need to walk in freedom.

Honor the Process:

Remember, this isn't about perfection—it's about progression. Some breakthroughs happen instantly, others take time. Some encounters are dramatic, others are gentle whispers. Trust the process and keep moving forward.

A Personal Word to You

I want you to know something: if God can reach me in my mess, He can reach you in yours. If a broken, angry, alcoholic mom who made terrible decisions can walk in the Courts of Heaven and experience daily intimacy with her Creator, so can you.

You are not too far gone. You have not made too many mistakes. Your family line is not too damaged. Your secrets are not too dark. Your shame is not too deep.

Jesus paid it all—every debt, every accusation, every legal right. The certificate that says "Debt Paid in Full" has your name on it. The keys to the Kingdom are in your hands. The garden of intimacy is waiting for you to come home.

The Invitation Stands

Eve lost the garden, but you don't have to. Adam fell from grace, but you can be restored. Generations have been bound by the same cycles, but you can break free.

Your Father is waiting to walk with you in the cool of the day. Jesus is standing ready to be your advocate in every court case. The Holy Spirit is eager to lead you into all truth and supernatural encounters.

The door to Heaven isn't closed to you—it's wide open. The question isn't whether this is available to you—it absolutely is. The question is whether you're ready to step through that door and discover what it means to live as the free son or daughter of the King that you were always meant to be.

Back to Eden

We started this journey asking questions about Eve, but we're ending it with an invitation to you. Come back to Eden, friend. Come back to intimacy. Come back to freedom. Come back to the garden where your Father is waiting to meet with you daily, to heal every wound, to break every chain, and to restore everything the enemy has stolen.

Your journey from bondage to freedom, from religion to relationship, from shame to honor starts with a single step.

And that step is simply saying "yes" to the invitation that's been extended to you since the foundation of the world.

Come home. Your Father is waiting.

Revelation 21:3-5

³ And I heard a loud voice from the throne saying, 'Look! God's dwelling place is now among the people, and he will dwell with them. They will be his people, and God himself will be with them and be their God. ⁴ He will wipe every tear from their eyes. There will be no more death or mourning or crying or pain, for the old order of things has passed away.' ⁵ He who was seated on the throne said, 'I am making everything new!' (NIV)

Your new is waiting. Step into it.

Stephanie

Description

What if you could experience Heaven right now—imperfections and all?

We've all caved to temptation. Again and again. Maybe you've blamed Eve for humanity's fall, or wondered why you can't break free from destructive patterns.

What if redemption is closer than you think?

This isn't your typical Christian book. This is the raw journey of a woman who made "horrific mistakes" and thought she was too far gone—until she discovered that God chases you in your messiest moments.

Through stunning journal entries of actual Heavenly encounters, you'll journey into the literal dimensions of Heaven—not through death or perfection, but through faith and the redeemed imagination God designed for intimacy with Him.

These aren't fantasies. These are real encounters with Jesus in the Courts of Heaven. You'll experience divine healing and discover that Eden—perfect communion with God—is as close as the nose on your face.

Ready to experience the Heaven that's been waiting for you?

About the Author

Stephanie Stanfill isn't your typical ministry leader. She's learned that the most powerful encounters with God often happen in the messiest moments of life.

A prolific seer with a gift for experiencing Heaven's dimensions, Stephanie has spent years discovering that God's love doesn't wait for perfection—it pursues you right where you are. Her journey from making "horrific mistakes" to walking in divine encounters has equipped her with a raw authenticity that cuts through religious pretense.

Stephanie's heart beats for one thing: showing others that Heaven isn't just a distant destination, but a present reality available to anyone willing to believe. Her encounters in the Courts of Heaven and intimate moments with Jesus have transformed not just her life, but the lives of countless others who thought they were too far gone.

Stephanie's message is simple: God's redemption is closer than you think, and His love is bigger than your biggest mistake.

To schedule an Encounter with Stephanie,
please contact us at:

stephanie@theredemptionofeve.com

www.theredemptionofeve.com

Published by:

Scroll
PUBLISHERS

A division of LifeSpring Publishing
www.scrollpublishers.com

Has God spoken to you about writing a book?
Let us help you!

www.ingramcontent.com/pod-product-compliance
Lightning Source LLC
Chambersburg PA
CBHW030006110426

42736CB00040BA/544